The Life of a Seal

Katie Smythe

Rosen REAL READERS

Rosen Classroom™
New York

This *is* a seal.

Seals like to swim.

They spend most of their time in the water.

Seals eat fish.

Seals have their babies
on land.

They teach their babies
how to swim.

Words To Know

baby

fish

land

seal